# Beyond the Horizon

BRUCE CONROE

Copyright © 2022 by Bruce Conroe.

ISBN 978-1-64133-862-2 (softcover)
ISBN 978-1-64133-861-5 (ebook)

All rights reserved. No part of this book may be reproduced or transmitted in any form or by any means, electronic or mechanical, including photocopying, recording, or by any information storage and retrieval system without express written permission from the author, except in the case of brief quotations embodied in critical reviews and certain other noncommercial uses permitted by copyright law.

Printed in the United States of America.

Brilliant Books Literary
137 Forest Park Lane Thomasville
North Carolina 27360 USA

This is dedicated to our children and grandchildren in memory of their mother and grandmother Barbara Holme Conroe, known in the family as Mom or Nina.

# Introduction

There are plenty of lands beyond the farthest we can see, hidden by the horizon created by the curve of this globe If you could walk to that point there is much to see. Many people are curious about the thousands of places on the globe but haven't a clear picture of what is there. It is very worthwhile to take advantage of any opportunities to travel and see what life is like in other countries beyond the horizon. Retirement is perfect for that. By then our children had finished their higher education and except for my mother the previous generation was all gone, as were some of our generation. We had time available, and finances were okay, so let's take a look at it.

This book was written for two reasons. One reason was to tell the stories of my many trips outside the United States for people who have never had the opportunity to travel abroad. The other reason is to give those who have travelled abroad the opportunity to relive some of those experiences and remember the people who travelled with them. The trips have mostly been voluntary except for the two biggest, one was forced by the Army Draft and the other I could not reject when asked to go by my boss.

I have been to 43 countries, some of them more than once and not always with the same companions. When traveling becomes safer, there may be more people taking a chance. It is very worthwhile to be somewhere where you don't speak the language but admire scenery and ancient buildings.

I hope my adventures are interesting to all readers. This is my second book. I previously wrote and published *Memories of a Reluctant Soldier: The Cold War Revisited*, which describes my experience as an Army draftee for two years. He was stationed in West Germany, which was under Allied control. Germany was split at the end of World War ll, with Russia controlling East Germany. My wife Barbara joined me, and our first child was born there.

My travel companions and I have visited some of the countries more than once. Those multiple visits are described in the years they occurred, which may be of interest when a country has changed between those visits. Several of the journeys included a cluster of neighboring countries. Many of these trips were guided tours.

Between the international trips we also took several trips in the United States, often using our timeshare swaps for housing.

# Chapter 1

## A TEENAGER'S FIRST FOREIGN TRIP AUGUST 1947

This was probably the shortest trip out of the USA anyone could take. I was 16 and travelled with my father to Montreal, Quebec, Canada. We flew up there from Albany, New York (no jets) in the morning so Dad could meet with important people in the University of Montreal's medical college to discuss steps needed there to obtain professional reciprocity for its graduates coming to New York State. Dad was an Assistant Commissioner of Education.

What to do with Bruce all day. A very compatible nun was assigned to show me around the University. She was very nice and enjoyed my thanks (merci) when steering me through the buildings. I had not yet studied French, the language in

Quebec Province. It was sobering to not have conversations with most people.

In 1947, Americans and Canadians could cross the border without a passport and USA money was satisfactory there. Years later My wife Barbara and I were in and out of Canada; by then, we had both studied French and could try it there.

After a quick lunch, my guide showed me the university's museum. Late in the afternoon Dad and I returned to the airport to fly back to Albany. Not long after takeoff, the pilots received a message that the Albany airport was socked in with heavy fog, too heavy for adequate vision in Landing.

This made me a bit nervous, not knowing how we would get there and at a reasonable time. The next day I was scheduled for surgery at Albany Hospital for removal of my tonsils. The airline told the pilots to land at Glens Falls, 50 miles north of Albany, and a bus would take us the rest of the trip. It worked well even though my mother and other people's greeters were tired of waiting for us.

The next day I checked into the hospital, and the surgery went well. Then I was told I would have to stay two nights, not one, because of my age. Tonsillectomies are more serious the older we get, and 16 was the lowest age that required the extra night.

Even though the trip was quick, the idea of learning about other countries, languages and politics stayed with me. I wished I had studied French.

# Chapter 2

## BY THE BLUE DANUBE RIVER JUNE 1955 TO DECEMBER 1956

Several years passed before my next foreign trip, but it was not something I had planned. After high school I attended Alfred University in southwestern New York and earned a Bachelor of Arts degree in mathematics. In 1953 I married my high school sweetheart, Barbara, and we lived in Alfred while I attained a Master of Education degree. We moved to North Syracuse, New York, where I began teaching Junior High (now called Middle School) math. That went fairly well, although I was 23 and looked 16. That Christmas of 1954, I received a US Army Draft notice to report for duty January 7, 1955, which I did. After refusing Officer Candidate School, which would have added a third year to my Army term, and after surviving two

two-month sets of Basic Training, I was sent to West Germany. This would be my longest foreign travel trip (19 months) ever. I arrived there with several fellow draftees I already knew, ending a long Atlantic voyage. Then we were on trains to go south to the state of Bavaria, giving us a lot of time to look at the gorgeous scenery and architecture. The landscape was filled with farms and churches that had steeples. In several small towns, children were getting ready to walk home from school with backpacks and wearing shorts. We were stationed at an Army base named Fort Skelly in Regensburg, in a Company I of the 6th Armored Cavalry . With other companies, we were guarding the German-Czech border. The Cavalry has no horses, but every man was assigned to a vehicle if the company were called into action. Ast the end of Basic Training we were broken up into smaller groups when we finished that program and we were scattered we were in three battalions. I was really lucky to establish a great friendship during Basic with another soldier named Bob and, through all the dividing, we both ended up in Fort Skelly in two companies next door to each other. Bob really saved me, having the same interests. me more about developing films that first summer. I was seriously missing Barbara, who was planning to come over the Atlantic when possible, and Bob missed his fiancé.

Regensburg is a medium sized city on the Danube River and is a major port. It is north of Munich and south of Nurnberg. It is picturesque and fairly ancient, having been established by the Romans in the 7th Century. As you drive into the city, the first thing you see is the cathedral with its two high spires leading your way to the center of the city. The spires each have a metal circle around them to hold them up during Allied bombing. In some buildings there are holes from earlier machine gun fire. But at noon each day most of the churches in the city ring their bells, a wonderful sound. The city is on the Danube and has always been a major port. There is an ancient bridge across the river in the center of the city that was built in the 11$^{th}$ century and is still strong while holding the many vehicles that cross it each day. The cathedral was also built in the 11$^{th}$ century and is amazing inside, but in 1955 it had nothing to sit on during Mass. There were many things to see in the city, which was great if you didn't have a car. The castle of the Thorne and Taxis family was open to the public. Outside of the city there was a memorial building of statues praising war heroes of long ago. Barbara came to Germany in September of that year, travelling on the *SS Stockholm*. We set up a modest home and met other couples. One of those took us on rides and helped us understand a lot. Our oldest son was born there on December 7$^{th}$ and winter closed in. Decades later we were told that the winter of 1956 was the coldest time in that century. In the spring of 1956, we bought a used car from a man going home to the States. That opened sightseeing doors for us. At that time the country had no equipment or food for small children in the hotels. Regensburg had a lot to offer, in things to see. There were the churches, museums and restaurants. Dinners out were very good and inexpensive. One dollar equaled 4 marks.

    For the USA Memorial weekend, we drove to Ulm in the center of Bavaria. We visited a high school classmate of both of us. He and his wife entertained us with a tour. We stayed in a hotel but were prepared with Gerbers food and the car bed for Scott. It was nice to get away from home. The countryside was beautiful. We saw acres of land growing hops for beer making. We also saw some storks flying in and out of their nests feeding the young ones. In the summer we took some time off to go to a military family resort in the Alps. While there we rode a tram to the top of one mountain one day and on another arranged for one of the resort's baby sitters and went on a cruise on Chiemsee Lake. We toured one of the castles of Mad King Ludwig, who had three of them. Salzburg was nearby but would have required special papers to go to another country. The Fort Skelly soldiers did not have a lot of chances for time off. That got even worse that

October with the beginning of the Hungarian uprising. Everything got serious. In December, Barbara, Scott and I sailed across the Atlantic on a US Navy troop ship to New York, and a return to regular living.

# Chapter 3

## WE ADD SOME MUSIC
## SUMMER 1985

This trip happened by way of an invitation. By 1985, our family of 4 children and our cat had moved to Potsdam, New York when I took the position of Counselor at the state college there. The Crane School of Music is part of the College and its choir director had planned a singing trip for former students to take place in England, Scotland and Wales. They needed another tenor (me) and an extra soprano (Barbara). This was a big opportunity, requiring us to rehearse for 5 days, pay our way and bring the right clothing (tuxedo for me and floor-length black dress for Barbara). I borrowed a tux from another Crane professor. The music was a mixture of classical and popular, our director Cal having been told that Europeans liked American musicals. Fifty singers and friends of ages 20 and up flew out of Montreal Airport on July 12th on our way to London. Cal's wife, Gail, who was also a music teacher, was in the group as was our accompanist. This would be 3 weeks of singing, starting in Shrewsbury, England, singing in competition with various schools. One men's school in Wales really was amazing. All of this took place in the Shrewsbury Cathedral's Abbey, which led us to really sing out. During the whole three weeks we were scheduled to stay with families, usually two of us to each host home. What a terrific way to learn more about the nations we were in. They provided breakfast and a box lunch plus transportation to and from the park where our bus picked us up. In Shrewsbury, Barbara and I stayed with a wonderful family with three children. Their home was large enough for all of us and fairly new. We had their guest bedroom and Esther (wife and mother) insisted that we take a tray with electric teapot, tea, jug (it is what the British call a pitcher) of milk and cups to our room for the next morning. That was great, just like being part of the family. While we were there, their son, Alexander, was notified that he was accepted to play his horn in his school's band in the fall. We helped them celebrate a teenager's good fortune. In the middle of our stay in Shrewsbury, our choir went over a short distance into Wales on our bus, where we gave an evening concert at a small country church. Everything went well after one problem. Cal stepped up on a wooden box to direct us. The box broke, throwing Cal. A fast tenor in the front row grabbed him and the concert started. After the program we were invited to the pastor's house next door, for refreshment.

I have never before or since tasted such delicious scones nicely coated with homemade jam. I should have warned you that, in many of our trips, something unplanned would occur for better or for worse. Next we went to lower Scotland by way of a scenic view of the Highlands. During all of the travel we visited interesting buildings and land, namely Warwick and Durham Castles. We arrived in Dunfermline, where Barbara and I stayed with a family of four with two quite young boys, Ross and Mark. It was still daylight at 10: pm. School there was still in session through July, so we asked how they got the boys to sleep earlier. They said they have black shades in their bedrooms which take care of that. We sang in churches while there and in Carnegie Hall. Yes, really. We also visited Stirling Castle. King James VI of Scotland and later James 1 of England, the son of Mary Queen of Scots, was born there. An amazing place, huge and probably cold with only fireplaces for heat. We also found time to visit the city of York, a fascinating place, we also visited Harrogate in Yorkshire. Next our solid bus drivers took us to the London area. We did a lot of sightseeing there, including the Tower of London and Westminster Abbey. We also watched the Changing of the Guard at Buckingham Palace. Barbara and I and another couple (Russ and June) were lodged with a single lady in Bromley, on the south of the Thames. Emmie was happy to have us and she was a lot of fun.

 Then it became time to fly home or, rather, to Montreal. Cal and Gail were on a side trip while over there, so I was in charge of overseeing the return trip. This was happening near in time to the plane explosion in Scotland at the hands of terrorists was so near the plane explosion in Scotland that

I had to make sure that everyone went through Customs and reports of purchases calmly and quietly. Of course, something had to go wrong. One young man had left his passport in the suitcase that had gone onto the plane. Luckily, he had a photocopy in his wallet.

One of the of the airport staff phoned the Montreal airport. They, in turn, said that the copy would suffice. After that, all went well.

What a wonderful experience!!!! A lot of us hoped that Cal would do another trip like this someday but with a strong box for Cal to stand on.

# Chapter 4

## HALFWAY AROUND THE WORLD
## OCTOBER 1986

This three-week trip to the Orient requires an explanation. I was then 55 and had told the College that I was retiring in August, and we would move from Potsdam in October. That July, the College President asked me to visit seven countries in southeast Asia with a group from 13 other colleges and universities to talk to high school students in American high schools in the capitals. Spouses could not go, and the College would pay for it. Barbara's reaction was that this was a rare opportunity, and I could not say no. She was always very good at backing what chances popped up, both those for my career and those for us. In early October we packed our belongings for storage while our house was being built on the outskirts of

Saratoga Springs, NY. We found a motel with cooking facilities for Barbara, and away I went, flying from Albany, NY. to San Francisco. At that airport, the group of 13 (mostly Admissions or student services people) gathered for extra reminders of things Oriental from our leader, Linda, of Linden services. Then we flew the rest of the night. There were stops in Hawaii, Tokyo, Hong Kong, Kuala Lumpur (Malaysia) and our goal, Singapore. We changed our watches often. What a beautiful, clean tropical city-state.

On the last leg of our flight, which was from Kuala Lumpur, I was seated in the aisle seat of three. Next to me was a young Chinese woman and her young child. At the window, sat a middle age Oriental woman. We all talked to each other in various languages with the lady in the middle handling it all very well. I will always remember that chance meeting along with many others from this trip.

In each of the seven cities we visited, we received a short reminder of the location after checking into our hotel. We visited American schools plus holding a college night at a hotel, and sometimes added a local school. In all seven cities, the students were happy to see us, especially for a chance to speak to English speaking people and practice that language. We also had sightseeing opportunities and times to learn to understand Asian meals.

Very exhilarating.

In Singapore, I had lunch one day with a Potsdam College graduate. Rosie had attended our school of music and was teaching in a Singapore music school. We met when she was at Potsdam, making it easy to catch up. In spite of the distance from home, she liked studying there. Next, we flew to Kuala Lumpur. Our pattern of activities was the same, but we were in a city we did not know much about. We had a wonderful visit to a Malaysian high school for boys. They welcomed us exuberantly, and we had a wonderful discussion with them. Very cheerful young men! On we went to our next stop, Hong Kong. After a nice flight we came down to the airport on an island in the bay and taxied along right next to the water where we could see some of the Chinese JUNKS that people lived in. A bus took us to our hotel by way of a bridge, but traffic was difficult because Queen Elizabeth II and Prince Phillip were in town and of course had the right of way in traffic. We went to a very nice restaurant in Hong Kong and learned more about how they served meals. For example, eight people sit around a circular table and each one would order a different main course. These were then placed on a central rotating board so that each person could take from whichever of the main courses he or she wanted.

Beside doing our meetings, there was a lot to do in Hong Kong. A trip to the top of the peak from downtown was especially exciting, we went up in an elevated tram and could see all across the city when we got to the top. We also could take a ferry boat across to Kowloon for shopping. I especially went to the jewelry stores to buy something for Barbara and the children. In one store I bought nice earrings for Barbara but didn't add the brooch that matched them. When I went back to the hotel my door would not unlock. At a friend's room I phoned for help and the manager came right up. They had secured my room because as I ran out the door earlier, I had not closed the small safe, and the cleaning lady had called it in. Ouch!

In shops and restaurants, we needed local currency, which meant finding currency exchange stores in the cities. We had been warned that when we left each country, we would need new currency at the next one. Therefore it was smart to use up the money in each country as we moved among seven nations. because they only swapped USA Dollars and not each other's money.

After our time in Hong Kong, our group took a train into Communist China. It was like being in another world. A young armed soldier sat by the tracks as security and looking very bored. An elderly lady came down the car's aisle pushing a tea wagon which was nice. We were on our way to Guangzhou (also known as Canton), which was exciting. We were warned that the hotel meeting would be over filled with people from fairly far away, because they wanted to hear about our institutions and practice speaking English. It was crowded, but we survived. I talked with a few who were looking for graduate programs. One woman was interested in Potsdam's music masters, was divorced and had money stored in Montreal thru relatives.

The next morning, I got up early to walk down to a park and watch many people doing the exercises. Later, we went to the station to take the train back to Hong Kong. The station was crowded, so a uniformed man pointed for me to go to a line for Chinese only. The Chinese in line yelled at me but of course I could not explain it. Oh well. The next day after we came back from China, I went back to the jewelry store and the girl who had served me before immediately knew who I was and what I was buying so I added the brooch to the collection. I also found jade tie clips for my sons. We liked walking+ around the streets. Often we met bird walkers (in the cages of course} and older ladies sitting on the sidewalk and sewing by hand.

Shopping in the various countries taught me a lot about the people. The salespeople were thoughtful, spoke English and were very polite. It was fun as a mathematician to stand there fascinated watching them total the bill with an abacus. Their hands literally flew over the wooden rings.

On we went to Taipei, Taiwan (Republic of China formerly Formosa) and not part of the People's Republic of China). People there were interested to learn more about the United States and our institutions, probably because there have been exchanges of students and professors from there. It is an independent country and a large island.

The gathering for our college night was much smaller than the others we had done and, therefore, more relaxed.

At this point, there were only two more countries for us to see. Seoul, South Korea was our next stop. We were surprised to see Americans there, forgetting that we still had a large number of military service men and women posted there. Being farther north than the others, Korea is colder. They have cleverly built underground shopping areas under the downtown streets. We visited the preparations for the Winter Olympic Games that were coming. During some of our free time I sat in my hotel room working on the list of chapter titles that I could use later in writing my book about my Army experiences which is titled *Memories of a Reluctant Soldier: The Cold War Revisited.*

Our final stop was Tokyo, and it was late *October* so a lot of attention in the United States was on the World Series. We enjoyed a tour of Tokyo, especially going slowly past the Emperor's Palace, even with a high wall. This, our last major presentation, was held meeting at St. Mary's School. Students were invited from 8 schools. Many of us were gathered in the gym when the winner of the World Series was announced. I think it was the Mets.

After this successful event, our group was invited to the school principal's home for refreshments, a nice way to end. The next day we flew to Los Angeles and then on to our homes. I was anxious to find out where Barbara was located 1) still in the motel and the house not finished, or 2) the house was finished but she was waiting anxiously at the motel, or 3) the house was finished and the furniture moved in. It was number 1. She was still in the motel and assisting welfare people housed there. She had also been to my parents' house for dinner a few times. She also kept an eye on how the construction of our house was progressing.

# Chapter 5

## MORE CHOIR MUSIC AUGUST 1989

This trip was another of Cal Gage's concert tours. They always started with rehearsals in Potsdam, a concert in Potsdam and then flight to central Europe. This time I had bought a tuxedo so didn't have to borrow it again. This time we stayed in hotels in Italy, Switzerland, Germany and Austria.

We landed in Amsterdam briefly and then to Munich, where we enjoyed beer and lunch in the well-known beer hall (Hofbrauhaus). Downtown Munich is amazing, especially the city hall (ratgerberlin.) Then, after some walking and meeting our guide, we left to arrive in Salzburg, Austria, to check in and have dinner. The next day we sang in a church. Often, we were the choir for a Saturday afternoon Catholic Mass.

Later we toured Saltzburg, especially spots where filming of *The Sound of Music* took place. We went back to the Vienna area for the night.

Before leaving the area to travel south, we were the choir in the chapel of a huge estate, Schloss Esterhazy. It is the home of the Esterhazy family. Composer Joseph Haydn and his family lived nearby. He was the organist in the chapel and is buried there. As we filed in for the service, we walked past his sarcophagus in the foyer.

We were located in the balcony and the family members were seated in a small balcony across the sanctuary from us. The same organ Haydn played was thrilling to hear.

Now were ready to leave Austria with our last activity the visit to a winery for a Heuregem (in German all nouns are capitalized) which is a party to celebrate the opening of a new wine. It was in Gumpoldskirchen.

# Chapter 6

## FAREWELL GORGEOUS ALPS

When we drove south into Italy we noticed it wasn't as clean as Austria. This area is the Dolomite Mountains. We stayed a few days in Cortina. From there we visited Venice. To get to the center of Venice we had to go on water buses. That was different. We saw glass makers at work and toured the canals. The gondolas are relaxing and quiet. We visited the Doge's Palace which is huge and gorgeous and St. Mark's Cathedral which is amazing. Cal asked the Priest if we could sing. He agreed as long as we didn't disturb the people praying. A few young singers were not allowed to go in. They did not follow the rule of not wearing shorts. A shame they missed it

On we went to Florence, one of my favorites. Seeing the famous statue of the Old Testament's David was a treasure.

Near it we checked out the shops on the well-known Ponte Vecchio.

We were staying in Montecatini, where we sang a concert in the Torretta's covered gallery. This interesting city is a spa with curing waters, pumped into a wall of faucets. From this city we visited the Leaning Tower of Pisa which is quite interesting.

On we went to Switzerland, Luzern particularly. We stayed in a hostel away from the city and reachable by boat. A big adventure was going up a high mountain (M. Pilatus) in a tram to see the view. The tram going up and the one coming down had to stop to get past each other. More concerts, restaurants and shops. I still have a wooden, rotating manger scene for Christmas and still in good shape. Another wonderful trip!

Now the whole tour is over. The choir went to Zurich to fly home. Barbara and I, and Cal and Gail Gage, stayed in Luzern two nights, then they went to visit someone elsewhere and we went to Amsterdam for two nights seeing artwork and the Anne Franck house before flying home.

## Chapter 7

## A DIFFERENT CLIMATE 1992

Barbara and I decided for a change of scene. We swapped our timeshare week at the Trapp Family Lodge for a week in the Caribbean. We had an apartment at a beach front resort on the island of St. Maarten. Lots of sand and lots of sun. It was interesting that the island is split down the middle with one side Dutch and the other side French. We were on the Dutch side, but of course we went back and forth between the two.

At one point we rented a car for an hour to drive to the top of the only high hill. What a view. We were very glad we had chosen this restful change.

# Chapter 8

## SINGING TOUR NUMBER THREE 1992

Yes, mostly the same crowd that had gone on the other two singing tours arrived for rehearsals in Potsdam and the final concert before we flew out from Montreal. There were some new people including my brother Bard (tenor) and his wife Jody(soprano). Cal had trouble adding tenors, so this was great. This would be the last of this series and we had the same guide as last time. His name is Norbert he is done Dutch and can speak at least four languages which is a great help.

This trip will include five countries with many concerts and lots of good times. From Amsterdam we traveled along the coast of the North Atlantic and visited a place where an elaborate system had been set up to hold back the water of the ocean. Sometimes it's hard to remember that Holland is below sea level. As we traveled, we stopped to see the delft factory which makes China which is blue and white. Next we went on to Belgium and stayed in Brussels, the capital. We enjoyed the people we met and the places where we sang and of course had to try the Belgium waffle. Delicious.

We traveled into Germany where we were expected to appear for a concert near Cologne. We were a few minutes late getting there but our accompanist sat down with the organist at the church out in the woods where we performed, and everything went fine. The city of Cologne had many things to see and is noted for its position on the Rhine River and its cathedral. Travelling south by boat, we visited the castle in Heidelberg. We sang outdoors there From Germany we travelled westward into France. We stopped in Champagne and had a nice tour at the winery of Moet et Chandon. Interesting and enjoyable. Next, in the city of Reims we were very interested to see the building where the World War II surrender was signed. Then we were on or way to Paris and I was glad that I had studied French in college.

Our hotel was in the southeast of the city's center, but we learned fast how to use public transportation. After breakfast each day Barbara and Bard and Jody and I would take snacks with us and go to the busy area. We had a tour of the Palace of Versailles, but could not go in Notre Dame Cathedral which was being readied inside for celebration of the Assumption.

For me, the big moments came when we rode on our bus up the mountain in the city, Mont Mart. We were the choir for the Saturday Mass and our accompanist played the organ in the Sacre Coeur cathedral. I was sure glad Bard had come. He and I were half of the Tenor section. I sat there not believing that I was in a building our French professor had described and I presumed I would never have a chance to experience.

Still travelling west we went to Calais and boarded the daily airboat (bus and all) to cross the English Channel and proceed to London. It was great seeing the White Cliffs of Dover as we neared the shore.

Barbara and I had been in London before as you saw in Chapter 3, but I could go many times. We toured the Tower of London, the Parliament buildings the Changing of the Guard and Westminster Abbey. At the Abbey, we sang at noon immediately after the moment of silence when all of the visitors and guides had to briefly freeze in place. After we sang the Abbey's guide led us out away from the mobs, through the path that the monarch uses at his/her coronation. Wow. On the way to Heathrow Airport to fly home we had a chance to see the grounds of Windsor Castle. Then back to the USA. My brother and sister-in-law thought this was a marvelous experience; we enjoyed travelling with them. I hope you enjoyed the three singing tours in Europe. They each have a fat photo album in my bookcase along with language books and books about nations. This is a good place to pause and recall the manner by which Barbara and I changed our usual approach for travels both out of the country and the many we have enjoyed in the United States. We followed the new approach for 28 years after our 1993 trip. It is amazing when unplanned events change life.

# Chapter 9

## BRUSSELS AGAIN 1993

At Christmas time in 1992, we of course enjoyed the cards that arrived brining us up to date with friends of many years. One of them came as usual from Barbara's college roommate of three years, Peggy, who told us that she and her husband David were living in Brussels, Belgium, for three years while he worked at NATO. They had brought furniture, a piano, dog and car with them and gave us their phone number over there. It dawned on us that they were there when we came through Brussels on our last tour. Reading between the lines in the card, I thought she seemed a little lonely where she wrote that we could visit her there. I suggested to Barbara that we ought to go since we had no trip planned and she agreed. I phoned and was happily received. We planned some dates for a week in April 1993. We had a wonderful week with them. Peggy was a great hostess and was learning to be a talented guide. In the middle of the week we four went by car and passed through Luxemburg to the Alsace region on the border of France and Germany. We walked into the very old town of Riqurwiihr to our hotel because cars are not allowed in that walled town. The name of it is German. Years ago, the Alsace was grabbed back and forth between Germany and France We were there two nights and on the way back to their house it dawned on all of us that could and did travel together and we should do more.

# Chapter 10

## WHAT A LIFE! 1994

You may be wondering what is next – Portugal. Barbara and I decided that to thank Peggy and Dave and we would trade this year's timeshare week for a week on the coast of Portugal. A lot of British people go there the way we use Florida.

We planned our flights for a week in May, then called Dave and Peggy to say, "We will meet you in Lisbon on May 5th." In a conspiring voice. When we four got together in our rented car in the rain (where are the wiper switches when you need them?), we hit the road for the south. The drivers there were all over the road. We established that Dave and I would take turns driving, with the one off-duty handling the navigation.

The apartment building was very nice, and we had two bedrooms and a spacious balcony facing the ocean. The facility was actually British, which was very helpful. After we got settled, I informed the group that we would probably get asked to a meeting about timeshares. I offered to go alone, but they wanted to learn more about it. At the end of the presentation, David asked if there were secondhand weeks available, the leader said yes, he had a two bedroom one in July for sale and Dave pulled out his credit card. That meant that in the future our two couples could put together two weeks at a time.

One afternoon we were treated to an outdoor cooking demonstration preparing Spanish paella, and spectators were invited to participate. Peggy jumped right in and learned a lot. We even got delicious samples.

We had a great time there, especially enjoying the beach both for swimming and walking. One day we watch a man painting scenic works and I bought a really nice one of a sail boat coming to shore. It has been on our household walls ever since. When we went home, we were quite pleased with the whole trip.

# Chapter 11

## A TWO-WEEK DREAM TRIP 1995

Choosing our next trip with our friends took real discussion. It had to be outside the United States due to Dave's NATO hitch; he could go to the US only 30 days in each year to avoid adding more taxes. That was okay with us. We decided on one week in the Canary Islands just off the coast of northern Africa and one week on the island of Majorca in the Mediterranean Sea. Both are part of Spain, adding to the intrigue and using our timeshares. It also caused us to have to stay two nights in Madrid between the two weeks. We survived that quite nicely but had to get used to going to dinner at 9:00 or 9:30 like the Spaniard's. A siesta would have helped.

Our island in the Canaries was Lanzarote, which was flat and dry. Peggy and Dave were a day late arriving. Their pilot overslept, which wasn't in our agenda. We took a tour, and the guide showed us hot spots in the ground. A bit of paper could start a fire easily and did. We had a nice apartment and activities. One day we went on a camel ride sitting in a wooden seat for two people. Another day, a local store sent models and leather clothing. For a show. They did not have male models, so Dave and I volunteered. Great fun. A few days later we went to the store. I bought a leather vest and Barbara bought a blue-gray overcoat.

In Majorca the resort was German. Nice restaurants there. We took a tour that included a visit to the monastery where Frederick Chopin spent his last years. We saw the piano he used as he composed.

We flew back to Madrid to return home. All four of us thought the differences between the two islands made it interesting and Madrid was a nice add on.

# Chapter 12

## LAKE DISTRICT ENGLAND AND THE SCOTTISH HIGHLANDS 1996

For our next trip with Peggy and Dave, we decided to go one week to each of the two places mentioned above. For the English Lake District, we went on a tour where we stayed for a whole week in a former country mansion that had been turned into a place where groups could hold training sessions. It was a wonderful location and great people running it. Each night after supper they explained to us the four choices for the next day, each one with its own guide. They ranged from simply sitting on the bus and looking at the scenery or going to a farm and seeing how they handled sheep or hiking through pretty difficult hills or a trip that included very difficult hills. Each night we would tell them our choice for the next day, then of course away we would go early in the morning and be back in the middle of the afternoon. These four choices for each of the next days were labeled a the easiest through D the most difficult the two women. The two women did A or B each day David D each day and I did C because I was having trouble with one knee. The whole week was wonderful.

Then we went with the whole group back to Manchester where we had started and people went off in their own directions. Our group had ordered arranged for a rental car and we were off to do Scottish towns by staying in bed and breakfasts. This was great, especially once David and I got used to driving on the left-hand side, one of the first ones we went to were on the west edge of the whole island and those people were so nice to us that we stayed three nights at that house. We went to a tour of a small castle on another island and sometimes we went into town for dinner and went to a pub for entertainment. They had somebody playing an accordion and somebody playing a violin and they were wonderful Scottish songs but we couldn't stay too long because of my smoke allergy and the smoke was sure thick in that place.

When we left there, we went further north in the Highlands, went past lake Lowman, and we visited castles along the way so we did a loop going way to the far north, each day we would stop and ask for bed and breakfast but you could organize it before you even left town. Each town had an office with somebody who would help us. In Manchester to get our plane, we also went through York and that was very interesting because we were able to see some ancient buildings that might have been in the Barden family way back – my mother's family.

After spending a night in our motel in Manchester we had organized them to drive us to the airport so away we went on time the next morning. But the driver of our cart that was taking us went to the wrong terminal first, so we thought Oh no we're going to be late, but he put us back in and the way we went to the right one and when we got there our seats had been given away already so they stuck us in business class we thought we had died and gone to heaven. Altogether it was a wonderful two weeks.

# Chapter 13

## MAJOR EXPLORATION 1997

At this point in our years of traveling, we decided did to tackle Countries that would be of interest with great histories to study. Therefore we signed up for a tour to have two weeks starting in Greece and then the Greek islands and then Turkey meaning Athens to Istanbul.

From Athens we visited many ancient sites. At the Parthenon our guide showed us the implanted rock at the entrance where St. Paul preached.

Next, we went by boat overnight through the Greek Islands. On Santorini Island we had a mountain to conquer to get to the village. You could go up on a tram or on a live donkey. Peggy refused the donkey BUT as we others got ready to be heaved on one Peggy was watching g us and got thrown on one. We laughed at that the rest of the day.

Our boat took us on to Kusadasi, Turkey, where we checked into a beautiful hotel. We also went to the village of Ephesus where Christ's mother, Mary, was taken for safety after the crucifixion. Another day we went to a rug-making company and saw beautiful products. Barbara and I bought one about 9x7 inches. Dave and Peggy also bought one and they gave us special bags to carry them home. Later Dave put his dirty clothes in that and the rug in his suitcase, all for safety in airports.

We flew to Istanbul, Turkey, with a very military guide who was armed guide. In Egypt, terrorists had taken over a cruise ship. They shot a lot of the passengers and pushed others into the ocean, including an elderly man in a wheelchair. We liked Istanbul after changing more currency and NOT drinking the water. We had been warned. Their finance system was crazy and out of control. Lunch one day cost millions of their units which I could not even calculate. Outside of the city we could see many large buildings never finished, but in the city we especially liked going to the mosque. We were really doing well with choosing countries.

# Chapter 14

## LET'S TRY THE WESTERN HEMOSPHERE 1998

This year we bravely planned two trips. The first one took us to the Caribbean Sea and to the island of Antigua. It was a chance to enjoy the sun and the sand for one week. More relaxing than sightseeing. We especially liked a boat taking us a few miles along the coast for good underwater viewing. That was fun. Actually, the event I remember the most was dinner the night before we left. It was out on a patio with flames for lighting. As we walked to it, we could hear a steel band playing beautiful classical music which went on to more plus popular music all through dinner. The second trip was in France, one week in the southeast part and Provence. We were really getting brave. Signed up for another walking up hills to classical castles. These were occupied by scared Catholics way back that the Pope wanted killed for their beliefs The castles' leaders could send information from one to the next from special towers for that purpose.

One woman in the group had also been in the hikes with us at the English Lakes District. Small world. After that week we went back to Toulouse airport to get our rental car and then drove east to Provence. We had arranged for a nice bed-and-breakfast. It was huge with one wing for guests and one wing for the hosts. Very nice hosts. He spoke English but she didn't but made a great breakfast. Three of us had studied French, which helped. Every morning our guide helped us plan where to go and what to see, especially the village markets. He did not want us to leave our expensive rental car in the street at night. He insisted that we use their garage and lock it. We visited churches, museums and the beautiful scenery. Then back to Toulouse to fly out.

# Chapter 15

## A WEEK IN MALTA 1999

This was a one-week tour with not much to do. Malta was a seaport of political interest. Its location on the Mediterranean Sea was important especially when wars were happening. The tour of the relatively small nation was interesting, and we enjoyed some boat rides, but nothing exciting.

In the same year ...

# Chapter 16

## LET'S TRY WATER WAYS 1999

Traveling friends had told us about how nice river cruises were. I called a travel agency advertised in a magazine and asked for a catalogue to be mailed. When the company representative asked if I had something special in mind, I told her we thought of the Danube with a stop at Regensburg, Germany. She said they had a tour that ended in Regensburg. We and our partners agreed on that one and made reservations. We also arranged for a hotel and a car at the end.

Everything worked out well, and it was good as predicted. First, we flew to Prague, Czech Republic, for a few nights. We tried the public transportation right away with success and walked around the business area of shops, offices and churches. There was a church downtown where we could walk in and lesson to free chamber music for a while. Nice. Our city tour was excellent.

Then we traveled by bus to Budapest, Hungary, with a problem getting through the corner of Slovakia. They were holding up a line of trucks and buses. Our first step was finding a shoe store. Barbara's sneakers broke down. Very successful. We also saw a statue of one of Peggy's ancestors. We were part of a group for another nice tour and went to the port on the Danube to check into our boat. The cabins and the rest of the ship and, later, the food was all terrific.

The next stop was Vienna, Austria, one of our favorites. Besides a tour and time to walk around, we saw where Mozart lived, toured the opera house and in the evening attended a concert in the Summer Palace. Going back to the ship we found it drifting away from the dock. New friends laughed at us from a window, but the ship came back in. There are many river cruises, and when they dock in the cities, they had to attack to each other because of lack of dock space. This river cruising is great. Unlike on the ocean, you always have a view and it is not packed since they are full with 125-150 passengers. We must do more of this. We sailed on into Germany to the island city of Passau. Very interesting architecture and easy walking. We were treated to an organ recital that was a treat. We were told that the organ is the largest in pipes in Germany.

The weather was great, the passengers were friendly, and every day was a learning experience.

Now are going on to Regensburg. Right away we see the cathedral spires and the ancient stone bridge that crosses the river and has since 1200 AD. Our hotel was nearby, we got our car and did not understand the public parking. A few days later we were invited to city hall with a fine since we didn't pay enough. I thought back to when (in Chapter 2) I went there to get our first son's birth certificate.

We drove and walked a lot. Peggy and Dave were intrigued that the city was founded by the Romans in the 800s AD. The cathedral had gained many chairs for the worshipers that were not there in 1955. The steel rings high on the spires for anti-bombing measures were gone. We attended Aunday Mass at 6:30 AM so we could see and hear the cathedral's boy choir. That was wonderful. The day after that we drove to Munich for our flight home.

# Chapter 17

## WHEN IRISH EYES ARE SMILING 2000

This was an invitation we could not ignore. Barbara and I were singing with the Skidmore College's Community Chorus of which the Conductor was fulltime at SUNY Albany University. One night he said that the Albany chorus was going to Ireland to sing in various places. He invited us to go if interested, at our own expense of course. We immediately signed up and persuaded my brother and sister-in-law to go. We would not be in the chorus but just going along for the ride. They were happy to go and I think having more people decreases the flight prices. We flew to Shannon Ireland airport and a bus took us to the hotel.

It was a really nice week. We enjoyed the singing and the sightseeing, never having been there before. We visited castles, the glass works at Waterford and Dublin. The latter of those had buses that drove in a circle in mid-town. You could buy a ticket to get on and off the bus wherever.

My greatest memory happened at night near Shannon. We went to a medieval castle for medieval meal served by women in medieval clothing. One man of the Albany bunch was chosen Lord of the Manor. He sent their conductor to the dungeon for some made up error. We had to eat with a few wooden utensils. All in all it was great.

Sometime during the week one of the women singers asked my to record their concerts. I was glad to do it. By the time we all flew to the U.S.A. she asked Barbara and me if we could be her grandparents. What next?

# Chapter 18

## COME BACK TO SORRENTO 2001

This was a wonderful trip with Dave and Peggy, including one week in the southern Italy area of Sorrento followed by one week in Tuscany up north. There was time to see Rome at the beginning. I seem to say "a trip was wonderful" quite a bit but it was true many times, and our partners agreed. We just clicked with them in all sorts of ways, for several years.

Of all the trips I am reviewing, this one in Italy had the longest list of subjects in my preparation notes to be mentioned. These are not in order they occurred, but the first group all happened when we were in Sorrento. That city was very friendly, and walking was easy to the shopping area. In one store we bought an inlaid wood side table which they would ship to our house and I bought a small wooden holder of tie clips And cuff links. That put us on their mailing list at

Christmas time and we received cards for a few years. One thing we did was to go to a family's house for lunch and when we got through the wooden Finch around the house we discovered a whole orchard of oranges and lemons and a separate building they had made for entertaining groups like us. They were very friendly the food was delicious.

Sorrento is on the Bay of Naples, which means we are in the view of Mount Vesuvius, and we could easily go over in that direction for reviewing that remains of ancient Pompeii. Very interesting. Another day we took us a small boat to the Isle of Capri and looked around there and noticed how pretty it was. Yet another trip was down the Malfi coast in our bus right along the edge of the ocean at the bottom of Italy. The road went very crookedly along the coast at one end; at one point our bus hit a biker and knocked him and his bicycle down. When the driver stopped the bus and looked, the boy was underneath the bus but he was not injured.

Some of the time we ate in restaurants when out on short tours. We found them to be really nice with excellent meals and low pricing.

At the end of the week our bus took us north into Tuscany and our hotel in Montecatini, a spa city with many faucets in the wall of a cave and each faucet having different water coming in to help with different physical problems people might have. One day a guide took us to the City Hall to meet the mayor. It was all very nice and relaxing. In fact, before we left we all in the whole group sang a piece from Aida and the opera written by Verdi. We sang The March of the Hebrew Slaves" one of the big favorites in the country. When Verdi was buried many people from the city formed a huge circle around his grave and sang this piece. Verdi was very respected by the people of Italy.

From Montecatini we were able to go to see the Leaning Tower of Pisa. The same day we also visited Florence where we had a sightseeing tour and went into the museum where Michelangelo's statue of David is located. We also did some shopping in the city square, which is huge, and I bought a leather jacket. Barbara bought some jewelry. I am sure Peggy and Dave were shopping also. We also visited Siena, a city with a huge annual horse race in the center of the city. Everything is wide open with the horses running over sidewalks and all. As the second week was ending, we rode to Roman and had a short tour around the Colosseum after a farewell dinner. The four of us sang (accompanied by Johnny). The melody was (Come Back to Sorrento) with words by me. At the end of alot of our trips I would write a poem about what we had seen there using some well-known tune. Fun.

# Chapter 19

## LET'S TRY RUSSIA 2002

This trip was a very nice river cruise from Moscow to St. Petersburg utilizing the Moscow River, miles of locks to the Onega Lake, stopping at small cities on the way. On Kizhi island there was a cathedral made of nothing but wood, no nails or other metal items. Next stop: west on the Volga River to St. Petersburg.

On the whole trip there was a terrific activities director who kept us busy. One day we had to take part in a musical show of strange characters that Peggy would not do. At the end the staff handed us a shot of vodka. It was all rather silly but fun. One evening balalaika players came aboard to serenade us.

I should mention that ahead of time we did not think the meals on the ship would not lack quality. They were great, and all the service on the boat was superb.

Back at the beginning in Moscow we saw Lenin's Tomb, Red Square, the Gum department store and the Kremlin. Of course, we did not try to go inside the latter. St. Petersburg was once the capital back when there were Emperors. We walked through the Hermitage Museum, which was originally the Winter Palace. It was so jammed with tourists that we just walked through.

Later a bus took us to Helsinki, Finland< for our flight home. On the way we stopped at a nice outdoor market of people selling a huge variety of items. I bought a pretty set of wine glasses.

# Chapter 20

## A TOUR IN THE WESTERN HEMISPHERE 2003

Mexico is very different from everything we saw in Europe. In Mexico City there was a lot to see and digest. The architecture is so interesting and old. Some of what we saw dated back to the Aztecs. We studied churches, .museums, galleries and government buildings.

Outside the city was flat, dry land with many pyramids and temples. Our ability to climb the pyramids improved each time we did it. We were on our way to Oxaca farther south. On the way we stopped in two villages and even met some of the people. They were very nice and pleased that we had come. We also drove through some beautiful hill country which made a welcome change from the flat land.

We flew to Mexico City for our flights north. Barbara and I had a major problem with that. When we landed in Mexico City they had just shut and locked the door on our plane without checking the number of people on board with the number of bags already on, including ours. They gave us tickets for the next flight to New York City but there was some waiting time, and the flight was going to JFK. The earlier flight with our luggage went to LaGuardia airport.

Everything went smoothly, even when we went to bed at our hotel at JFK. The next morning at 7:00 there was a knock on our door. It was a nice young man with our bags. What a relief. Driving home was easy. Peggy and Dave were on a flight to Newark so their trip went as it was expected.

# Chapter 21

## WHERE YUGOSLAVIA WENT 2004

This particular travel event needs a tiny history lesson. After World War II, six small republics were put together to form Yugoslavia with Josip Tito as its head. In the early 1990s, after Tito's death, the former republics returned to independence. Our trip included Slovenia, which is the farthest north, and Croatia the next one south of that. All six republics lie along the Adriatic Sea on the northern edge of the Mediterranean Sea.

We flew into the capital, Ljubljana and were there for several days. It was very relaxing in a country where all are happy and finances are not a problem. I asked our guide Matt how it could be calm while Croatia next door was struggling. He said that the leadership of Slovenia saw that freedom was coming and really prepared for it. One highlight there is Lake Bled – not large but very tranquil.

We enjoyed a boat trip to Kirk Island just off the coast which is an excellent spot for the large monastery there.

Next our tour group headed south to Croatia. Its capital is Dubrovnik, a large city right on the coast of the Adriatic. We did a lot of walking in the city to see the older buildings and a soccer field or two. The people were nice but still a bit tense in discussing their fairly recent war with Serbia, the next country south. One day we had a trip to Splitz Island. The biggest event was our dinner with a family. Their house and farm were very high up a steep mountain. We thought we might need to get out of the bus to give it less weight. It was having trouble the last quarter of a mile. We were with a very friendly family who had many questions about us and our country. They were happy to tell us about the war and about their family. A great meal, too.

# Chapter 22

## OFF TO SOUTHERN ASIA 2005

This was our 20th trip with Dave and Peggy including the ones we did with them in the United States. We were still close friends and excited about future travels. This tour of Thailand (formerly Siam) was spectacular as you will see. This tour had the longest list of activities of any tour and that is without me including a few minor activities. After flying 21 hours we landed in Bangkok and were taken to our hotel.

We met our guide for the whole trip and met with him after dinner – all 30 of us. His name was Udom, and he had spent a school year as an exchange student way before this. He lived with a family in Granville, New York, near the Vermont border. He was in high school. Now he looks 20 but is probably 35.

Udom told us that the middle name of his tour company was Adventure, and he was always on the lookout for unusual activities. One day that included leaving the bus at a farm to cut a crop of rice. Many houses we saw while touring Bangkok Had a tiny model on a pole to help their ancestors, spirits come home. Another interesting was spent buying clothing from the floating markets in the rivers of downtown Bangkok.

We packed up and left Bangkok headed northwest passing the bridge used in the movie *The Bridge on the River Kwai*. We went on to see the area when British troops were turned into slaves to the Japanese, who had conquered that land. We saw where they had been forced to dig a huge path through rock for the train track wanted by the Japanese. We also saw memorial plaques and a huge cemetery where they died from starvation and torture.

From that we went on the train there and got closer to our next hotel that was afloat on the river. It was tricky getting from a smaller boat in groups of 8 onto that fascinating atmosphere. We continued northward to Chang Rae. We were there for a few days, touring the area going across the border to see a tiny bit of Myanmar (formerly Burma). A nice young man drove Barbara and me around in his tuktuk which was like a small golf cart. We were told that any tip we gave would feed his kids for a week---so we tipped him of course.

Back in Chang Rae, I had left small photos of five of our grandchildren with an artist to sketch in ink . I had been told of this possibility back home. The sketches were perfect.

Now things got really exciting. We went to Chang Mae to visit the elephants in their training camp. We rode them in a seat for two and Barbara was aghast when our boy leading us motioned to me to get out of the chair and onto the massive animal's neck. He indicated how to direct the elephant with your knees behind those big ears and I did it with Barbara laughing wildly. Hooray. Next, we went floating down a river at the camp, with four of us on one raft. Barbara and Dave each tried to steer it. What a day. At day's end we loaded onto a train with sleeping cars to head back to Bangkok. We were given a boxed supper, and each assigned a nook that was twin bed size, and had thick curtains and a wall lamp inside. Wonderful.

Throughout the tour we marveled at the beautiful temples and the Thai people we met were very friendly. One morning we had been urged to get out of bed very early to go to a nearby neighborhood to pass out food to people. Children were all running around us, and it was a happy time for everyone there.

This really was an amazing experience that all of us in the group realized, too.

Now we are ready for the long trip home and that list can go into this trip's photograph and printed mementoes album, as was done with all of our trips. They have been at hand as these descriptions were written.

As we all were leaving, Udom handed out booklets of labelled photographs that he had put together for us using photos of the individuals receiving them. What a terrific friend and guide. P.S. Our two children whose five children were in the two paintings were thrilled when they saw the framed outcomes of our October trip at Christmastime.

# Chapter 23

## IF WE COULD SPEAK SPANISH 2007

Costa Rica is a small country in Central America, between Panama to the south and Nicaragua north. Our guide there told us that it is the only country that has no army. We flew into San Jose, the capital, where our travel agency's bus took us to our hotel. The next day we had a tour of the city, and it was nice being among palm trees. Later that week we rode through the country, stopping twice to see various buildings.

We went on farther to the northeast corner of the country. We checked in to a ranch covering many acres of land. Instead of rooms there were cabins for two people. For the next days there were several things to do. We rode horses through a jungle to get to the high altitude where a zipline started. Yes, we rode the line above many trees, coached by young men to help if needed. It was great. Afterward we could change to bathing suits and unwind sitting in hot springs.

The ranch bordered the Pacific Ocean. Above the water level there was a bar and a row of chairs. Our guide rounded us up to sit staring at the ocean while the sun sank which was quite an experience. In our group a woman named Jane was an artist. Everywhere we went we could see her sketching. About a month after we were home from this trip, Barbara and I received a package in the mail. We were surprised to find that it was a small oil painting of a sunset over water and a row of stick figure people watching plus a greeting card from Jane. Wonderful.

When we left the ranch, we were heading south along the coast. When we stopped for lunch, it was discovered that something was wrong with the bus. Our guide made phone calls to see what to do. She was instructed to put us all on public buses to a certain meeting place. What an opportunity to see the people close enough that we could talk, but Barbara and I did not speak Spanish. We exchanged smiles with the lady and her son sitting next to us. We visited a school where children danced and sang for us.

We then returned to San Jose and the next day flew home. What a great trip!

# Chapter 24

## A DIFFERENT PART OF ITALY 2008

Preparing for this trip to Sicily required some special attention as Barbara's Alzheimer's disease was of course getting worse. For the Costa Rica trip I had prepared a deck of index cards, each carrying details for a day's activities and the hotel's address in case she wandered. It worked well so I did that for Sicily too and took several T shirts of very bright colors so she could always see me in the crowd.

Sicily is a very large triangular island at the toe of the Italian boot with the city of Palermo for its capital. During our stay we visited many churches and more ancient buildings than I expected. At one point we went to the west end of the island to see a winery. We also visited Catania on the eastern edge of the island. In 1943 this island was very important in World War II when the American army landed there.

One day we went to see Mount Etna, a volcano on the eastern side. We hiked the whole distance to the top and were amazed at the view. I believe it erupted a few months later with huge columns of fire photographed for the news agencies.

I wrote another poem about our trip, to be sung to the tune of Mario Lanza's "Funiculi Funicula", which our foursome performed at the farewell dinner. We had really nice food and wine the whole time we were there. We also heard our guide say that Tunisia would be open to tourists the next year. When we got home, we and Dave and Peggy quickly made reservations. We were lucky because a few years later it was closed again due to political difficulties there. Friends on the Sicily trip we had met on other trips did the same so we looked forward to seeing them in Tunisia. We also stayed in contact with people we met on this trip.

# Chapter 25

## NOW WE ARE GOING TO NORTH AFRICA 2009

Tunisia turned out to be like being in Wonderland in the same way that Thailand had done for us. It was so unique with mosques, desert, camels and places where the movie *Star Wars* was filmed. The film company had come into the country and gone to an area of homes and a hotel carved out of solid sand. We even went into the hotel, which was still in business.

One day after visiting shops and a mosque we were told we would be on our own for eating lunch. At the last moment our guide, Mohammed, said, "Get on the bus, we're going to my parents' house for lunch." What a nice surprise. They were super nice people with a gorgeous home and a great cook.

Another day we went to the Sahara Desert. What a treat! We went where the camels were kept and each of us was assigned to one of them. We were given a wrap to cover our clothes and told how to get on the camel. Barbara loved it and obviously knew what was going on. Each camel had several rugs on its hump to make it comfortable and we each had a boy leading the camel on a rope. As we rode a few miles we wondered if this was really happening or were we dreaming. That whole time was just plain unbelievable. A visit to the U.S. Army Cemetery was serious enough to wake us up.

Barbara absolutely loved this entire adventure. She was understanding and remembering less of what was going on, but happy. It occurred to me that this might be her last major trip, and Peggy and Dave saw that coming too.

Our group was splitting, with some of us heading home and the rest staying for extended camping in the desert. Our foursome was in the first group. When we got to our final hotel we discovered we had especially nice large rooms, so Barbara and I hosted a wine get together in our room before dinner. It's amazing when recalling the events of that adventure.

# Chapter 26

## BACK TO THE RIVER BOATS 2011

For our next trip all four of us agreed to a cruise on the Elbe River in what had been East Germany after the war. We flew in to Hamburg, Germany, and boarded the ship there. We would be travelling south toward the Czech Republic.

Before starting the trip we had a tour of the harbor by boat and a visit to the Miniature Wonderland amusement park. There were just three of us. At the last minute, Barbara's doctor told me she needed to go into a facility – no more trips.

The place she entered told me not to come to see her for two weeks while she was getting settled, the exact length of time of this cruise. Our travel agency was very understanding and returned the cost of her trip. Of course she knew nothing of this and would have been confused if we tried to explain it.

Very sad after having a very bright brain, four children and 58 years of a happy marriage.

All river cruise vessels are superb, including this one. We cruised past five towns before reaching the Czech Republic. One of them was Wittenberg where Martin Luther lived and taught. He and his wife turned their house into a boys' school. Very interesting to see. We also spent time in Dresden touring the factory where, of course, Dresden China is made. In towns we noticed that people in East Germany Had less spectacular household and auto items. However that country had reduced the coal they could have shipped to West Germany during the Cold War.

As we travelled, the River kept getting smaller until it was too shallow for our boat. The tour continued by bus to Prague. There we toured part of the city that we had not done when there before.

This was a nice trip but not as exciting as some of the others. Perhaps my concern for Barbara played a role.

# Chapter 27

## IRISH EYES ARE SMILING 2012

Conroe is an Irish name. We had early Conarroe or Conro ancestors come to America, and my paternal grandmother (an Irwin) came from County Armagh, now in Northern Ireland. To help our current family perk up, I invited them all to go with me to Ireland (but we couldn't go to Northern Ireland). Using Google, I found a large and very nice house to rent in Kilkenny.

Eleven children and grandchildren signed on.

A bus I had arranged took us to JFK airport on a nice June day. We landed at Shannon Airport in Ireland, and we picked up the two vans I had reserved.

With son John and son-in-law Jim driving, we found our way to the house. It was perfect. We had no agenda but discussed what to see. One day to the coast, one day to Waterford to see the glass factory and one day to Dublin.

They all loved it. The only bad news was one granddaughter developed gastric problems and needed help at a nearby aid station. She was not able to go on the Dublin trip so I stayed with her while the rest went. Two days later she was okay and back into sightseeing, including the Blarney Stone, which required a major climb in the tower leading to it..

The weather was great for walking. We added the Cliffs of Mohr to our "to see" list even though it was a fair distance away.

To get a 5:30 am flight at Shannon we went to a hotel that night. I was surprised to find I could order breakfast for the middle of the night for all of us.

When we got to JFK on a Saturday the pickup area was jammed with vehicles. My state trooper grandson finally got our driver on the phone and it all turned out well.

# Chapter 28

## BUDAPEST TO THE BLACK SEA 2013

This trip was first planned to be Kiev, Ukraine, to the Black Sea. It is strange that I am writing when Russia is invading the Ukraine. Our travel agency cancelled our trip because the Ukraine decided to charge them one million dollars for using their waterway and wanted Ukrainians added to the ship's crew. The agency would give back our money or transfer it to the trip above and add $500 for the trouble. The extra cash gave us the extension trip in the north of Romania.

This year began with two overpowering events My beloved wife Barbara died in January and my right knee was replaced in March. I was glad for the upcoming travel plan for Budapest to Bucharest to be followed by Count Dracula's territory named Transylvania.

After getting settled in our cabins aboard ship, I walked along the sea wall looking for "the shoes". There are about 50 lined up where Jews were forced to stand facing the water with their shoes off. Then they were all shot by Nazi soldiers and their bodies fell in the water. Some were small children, as shown by the shoes. After the war the Hungarians had the shoes coated with metal and permanently lined up and solidly attached to the stone wall surface.

In Budapest, departing boats leave in the darkness of evening when the harbor comes alive with lights. We saw that the next day, watched a great horse-riding show and next began sailing through countries that had made up Yugoslavia. The first was Croatia where we had a home-hosted lunch.

We visited small towns as well as cities thru Bosnia and Montenegro and into Romania. In some towns there were small workshops where people made souvenirs that we were happy to buy.

Bucharest is a very large capital. There were many buildings to see as well as the outdoor spaces that formed a battle zone when they overthrew the leadership. Besides our regular guide, she had located a young man who had been in the battles and could tell us about it. He was about 12 back then and was still upset when his 12-year-old best friend was shot and killed in the fighting. He showed us a Romanian flag that was badly damaged but helps him remember. We had a good city tour there and also in Constantia on the shore of the Black Sea. When the whole tour ended some people went home, but we and others were registered for travelling northward to Transylvania. That was a very nice bus ride ending in a mountainous area much like the Alps. We had a very acceptable hotel and a lot to see around the city of Sinai. There were several palaces but the most interesting were the one with a hidden staircase to run up two flights and fend off whoever was attacking and the gruesome castle of Vlad the Impaler.

This trip was very worthwhile. I could not get over the number of countries we visited in a section of the world to which we had never been. Oh, I should mention that there were a lot more homemade trinkets available.

# Chapter 29

## LET'S TRY SCANDINAVIA 2014

This chapter starts with another shock: Our little group had shrunk again with Dave's death. We were registered for a tour in Finland and Norway. A few weesk before our date of departure, Dave took a nap after tennis and lunch and did not wake up. Peggy called for help and the doctors decided to operate on his brain, which was bleeding inside. There was no response from Dave and nothing more to do. He died a few days later. In a few days he would have turned 82.

    The agency we were using for our trip gave Peggy a YES. One of her daughters, Melissa, could take Dave's place. What a relief. We flew to Helsinki, Finland, staying there a few nights. We visited government buildings and a memorial to composer Jean Sibelius very nicely done with likenesses of his head created in aluminum. Near it was a church, most of which was underground. When we left, we flew above the Arctic Circle into Ivalo in Lapland. There were reindeer farms here, but it looked like a national park. The government built a huge dining room on one farm so tourists could be served. It was very nice and Reindeer meat is rather good.

After a few days there we boarded the King Harald, a massive Norwegian ship. It travels up and down Norway's west coast, delivering food, building material, mail and people. Folks could put their car on board or just plain walk on board. It had nice cabins and delicious food. It would dock at each town and we would stroll around. One afternoon as we crossed the Arctic Circle, there was a small celebration for that.

One night I woke up at about 1:30, hearing thumping noises. I looked out my porthole and saw stacks of lumber that were being unloaded. We were on the ship until it arrived at Bergen. The next leg of our journey included travel by fjord boat and train across the narrowest length of Norway. There was lots of beautiful scenery. In Oslo we walked through a very large park with many statues of nude people. We visited a museum of Viking boats and rafts including one raft that broke distance records years ago. It was the *Kon-tiki,* explorer Thor Heyerdahl's papyrus boat made famous in the 1960s.

# Chapter 30

## REGENSBURG AGAIN 2015

In honor of our son Scott's 60th birthday, he and I went to Germany so he could see his birthplace – Regensburg. We flew to Munich, picked up our rental car and headed north. I had forgotten how to handle driving on the Autobahns with no speed limits, but I caught on.

Our hotel was in the ancient part of the city and only one half block to the Danube River. We could walk to many things to show Scott. In the downtown square he saw the shop where we bought baby clothes and furniture, across the square from the old City Hall (Rathouse). We of course went in the Cathedral and studied all of the very old buildings in that area. We drove to the edge of the city to see all that is left of the US Army base -- just two buildings surrounded by a fence. We only found it by asking at the University (which was not there when Barbara and I were).

We searched for the last house we lived in when Scott turned 1, but could not find it. We did find the first place where Barbara and I lived. The road was dirt in 1955 but paved now, and those houses all looked better than they did right after the World War II. The small military hospital still looked the same. That night we walked from our hotel back to the City Hall. We had dinner in its basement, the rathousekeller. Another day we drove to Saltzburg, Austria, and looked around. We stayed there one night and drove back to Munich for two nights before flying home.

Scott wanted to see one of the Nazi prison camps. We went to Dachau. It had all been rebuilt, which made it less emotional until we went into the museum. Very moving! We also looked around downtown Munich and watched the puppet-like figures parade in a circle high above the street and built into the City Hall wall: the famous Glockenspiel.

# Chapter 31

## WHAT A LIFE 2016

This year I tried to find a companion for a cruise. Peggy was not feeling well, and others had plans. I decided to go alone and make friends on the boat. In this cruise everything happens at or near Bordeaux on the west coast of France. At the last minute my daughter Laurie said I should not go alone. Then she said she could go. So that is what we did and it didn't hurt that she is a nurse.

After a tour in Bordeaux, the rest of the cruise was 10 days of leisure. The boat took us up one of the three rivers that met there. This tour was called "Wine, Wineries and Chateaux". We visited all three. I told Laurie there were no assigned seats for meals, so we moved around, meeting new friends. At one table for dinner se sat with two French ladies. They had been childhood friends in Paris. Delightful people, so we ate with them many times.

On the daily trips we often toured vineyards. One was on the grounds of a huge, beautiful chateaux where dinner would be served after we walked through it. The fairly young owner and his wife had inherited the chateaux and its vineyard.

This was totally amazing and I didn't even mention activities in the evening. Sometimes it was dancing competition and Laurie lured me into that. Fun!

I was so glad that I had chosen this cruise that goes nowhere. Very restful.

# Chapter 32

## BAGS OUT AT SIX 2019

This year I couldn't decide what to do for a foreign trip and finally picked Scotland. Who would go with me? Peggy was no longer able to travel so I invited my immediate family and got yeses for 13 of them. With help from AAA, I found a tour group in London named Trafalgar that had many tours. I decided on a 10 day tour by bus from Edinburgh to Glasgow. Preparation was a big job including getting facts about each person and telling my AAA contact who would share hotel rooms. We were dealing with two of my children, three of my grandchildren and their significant others, four great-grandchildren, and one niece.

I hired a car to tick us up at my house, at which time I gave a short lecture on how to travel. That included being on time everywhere and paying attention to when our bags were outside the door for loading the bus. We had an amazing bus driver who looked very young but really knew how to handle a bus and 30 people. As usual we had been added to a group of people who had signed up for this. They all enjoyed trying to figure out how we were related.

We flew into Edinburgh, met the rest of our tour group and our driver and drove to our hotel. We were there two nights and toured the castle, saw the building that may have inspired the Hogwarts School in the Harry Potter movies and books, and saw coffee shops where JK Rowling did much of her Harry Potter stories writing. We also went to a wonderful dinner and entertainment with bagpipes and dancers. When they came among our tables to choose people to dance with them, grandson Ryan was chosen and had a great time. As we drove north the next day we stopped to see the famous St. Andrews golf course and several miles later toured Blair Castle.

Pitlochry was one of our stops as we arrived in the Highlands for two nights at a country inn. From there we visited Colloden battlefield, important in English history. The English army defeated the army that the prince Bonnie Prince Charlie had in order to gain the English crown. He escaped being killed by fleeing to the Isle of Skye. We took a dinner cruise around a nearby loch.

Then we travelled south and saw Loch Ness on the way. Farther south we were impressed with the huge size of Stirling Castle, where Mary Queen of Scots lived when her son was born. He later became James VI of Scotland and James I of England.

We arrived in Glasgow and checked in to our hotel. Everything about this tour was working very well. My whole group was having a marvelous trip. My granddaughter's family of six found several museums to visit in the cities when we had free time. Our bus took us on one more adventure. We went to a 15$^{th}$ century farm where the family served a great meal and entertained us with singing. After eating our total group was divided in half to form two teams singing in competition for a bottle of wine. Our group won and I was the receiver of the reward – a tiny bottle of wine, a few inches long.

The trip to JFK Airport went well and all fourteen of my family group took away many happy memories.

You may ask if my travelling days are through. No. I found a new companion who had not travelled overseas. Wally and I had both lost our wives, so this has worked. This spring we will take a river cruise in the USA. We introduce ourselves as "The Wandering Widowers". We make a good team at ages 91 (me) and 80(Wally). I hope you enjoyed my adventures.

With many thanks to my proofreader, Judy Eckman, for a great job.

### BRUCE A. CONROE ED.D